To my children,
Alan ,Lewis & Emily
Always believe in yourself!
Love from Mum.

To our cat Minnie, Thank you for
all of the love and inspiration to
write this book.

This book belongs to

....

First Published in 2024
text and Design copyright © Jenna Mcatamney

Minnie The Cat

Once upon a time, there was a little black cat called Minnie.

Minnie lived with her family in a beautiful home with a big garden.

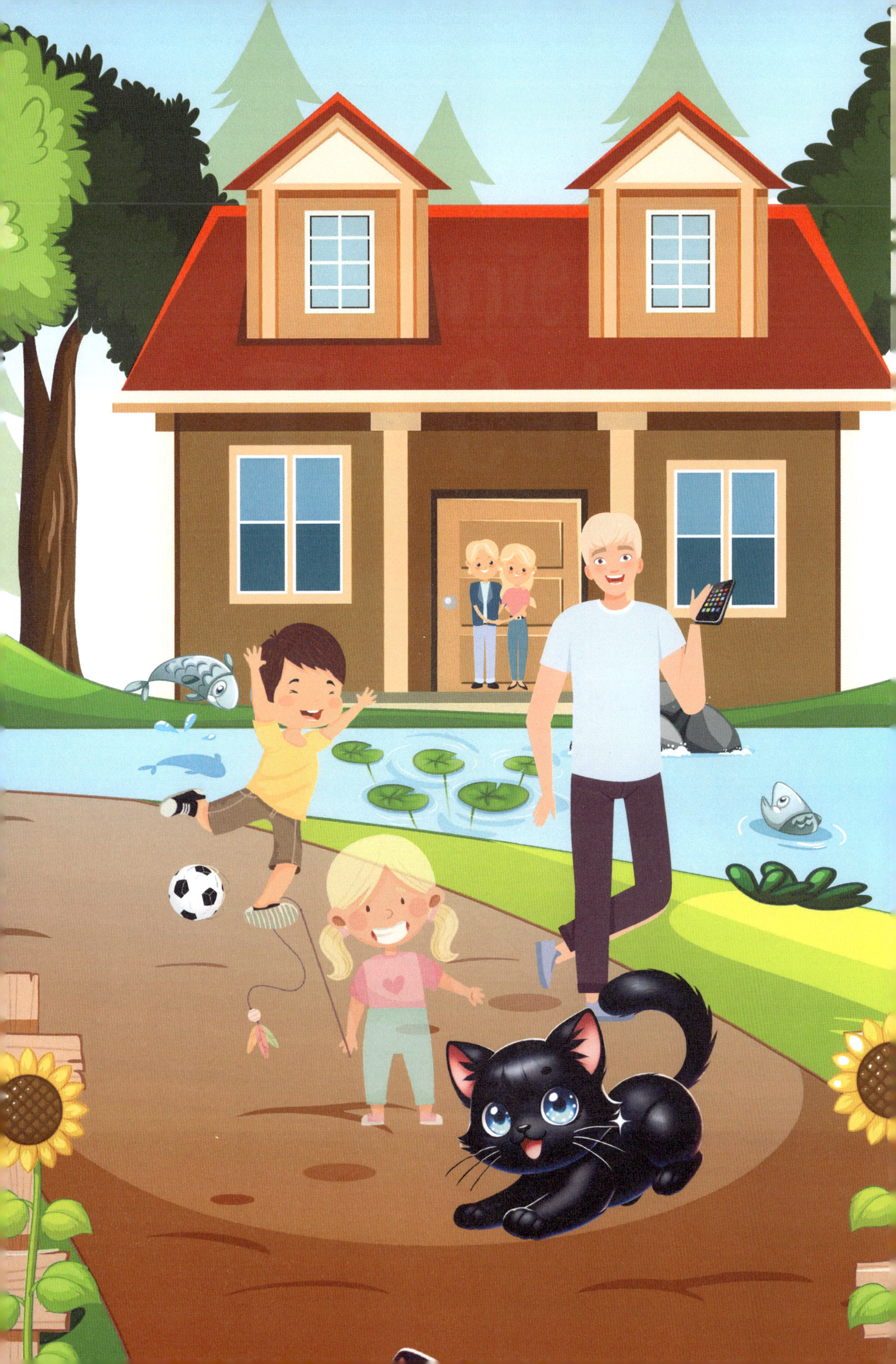

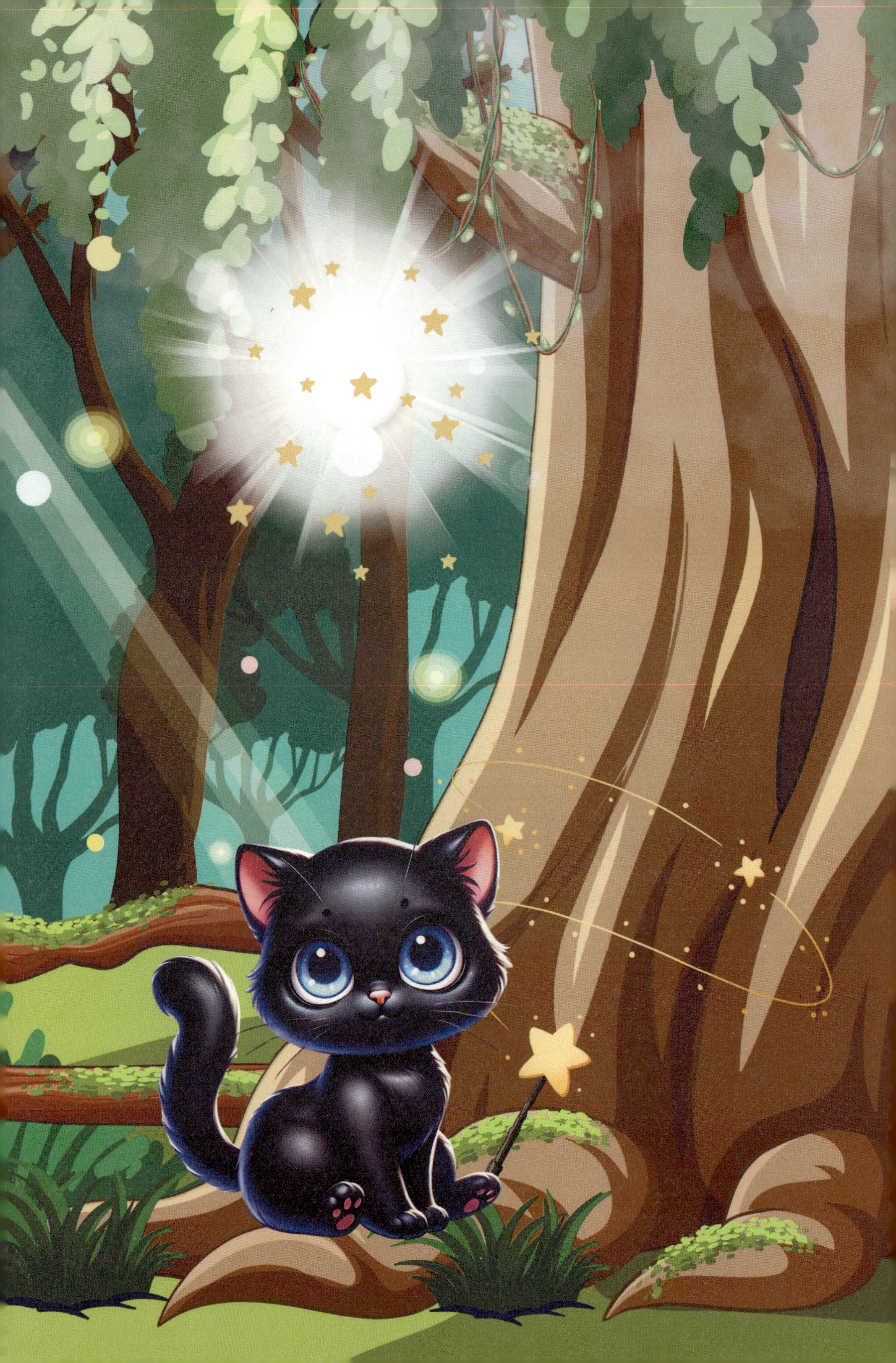

Everything seemed ordinary, YET Minnie was extraordinary, she had MAGICAL powers.

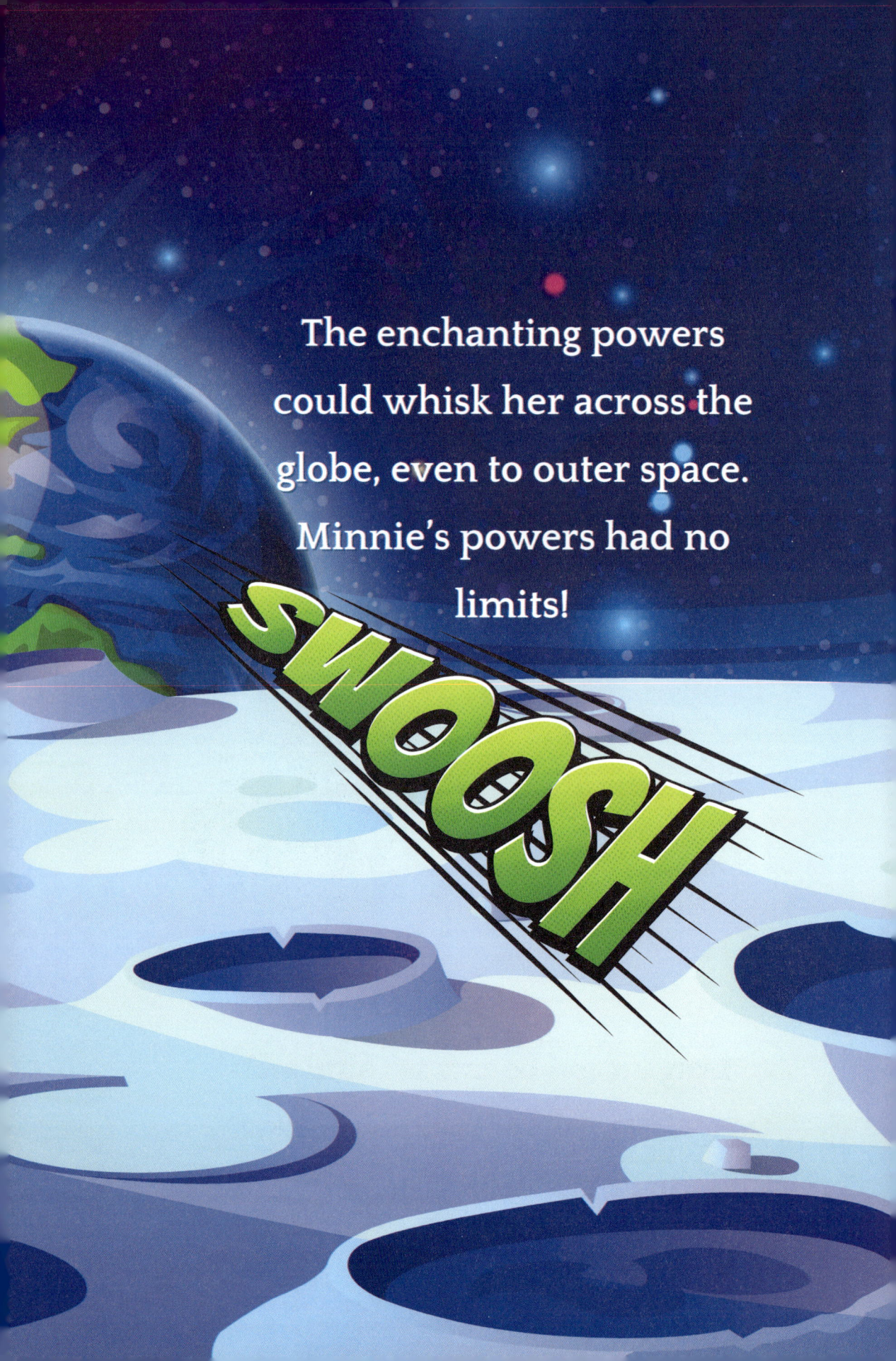

The enchanting powers could whisk her across the globe, even to outer space. Minnie's powers had no limits!

SWOOSH

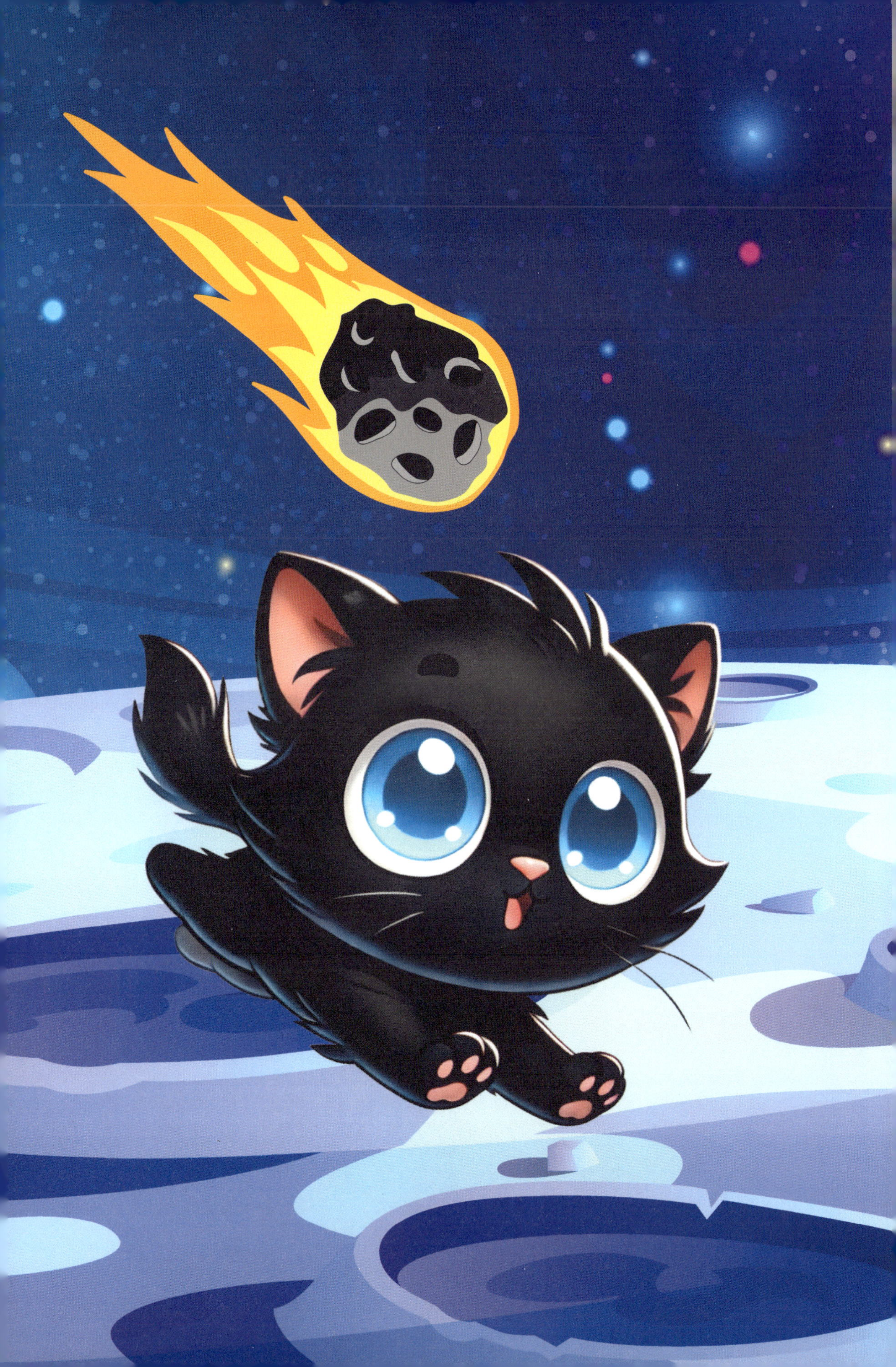

But how did Minnie unlock her special powers? , A huge burst of imagination from her marvellous mind , a sprinkle of magic, kindness and her favourite toy.

Once the ingredients were mixed, the magic came alive! Her favourite toy was now a MAGICAL wand.

Minnie discovered this power when she was just a little kitten playing at home.

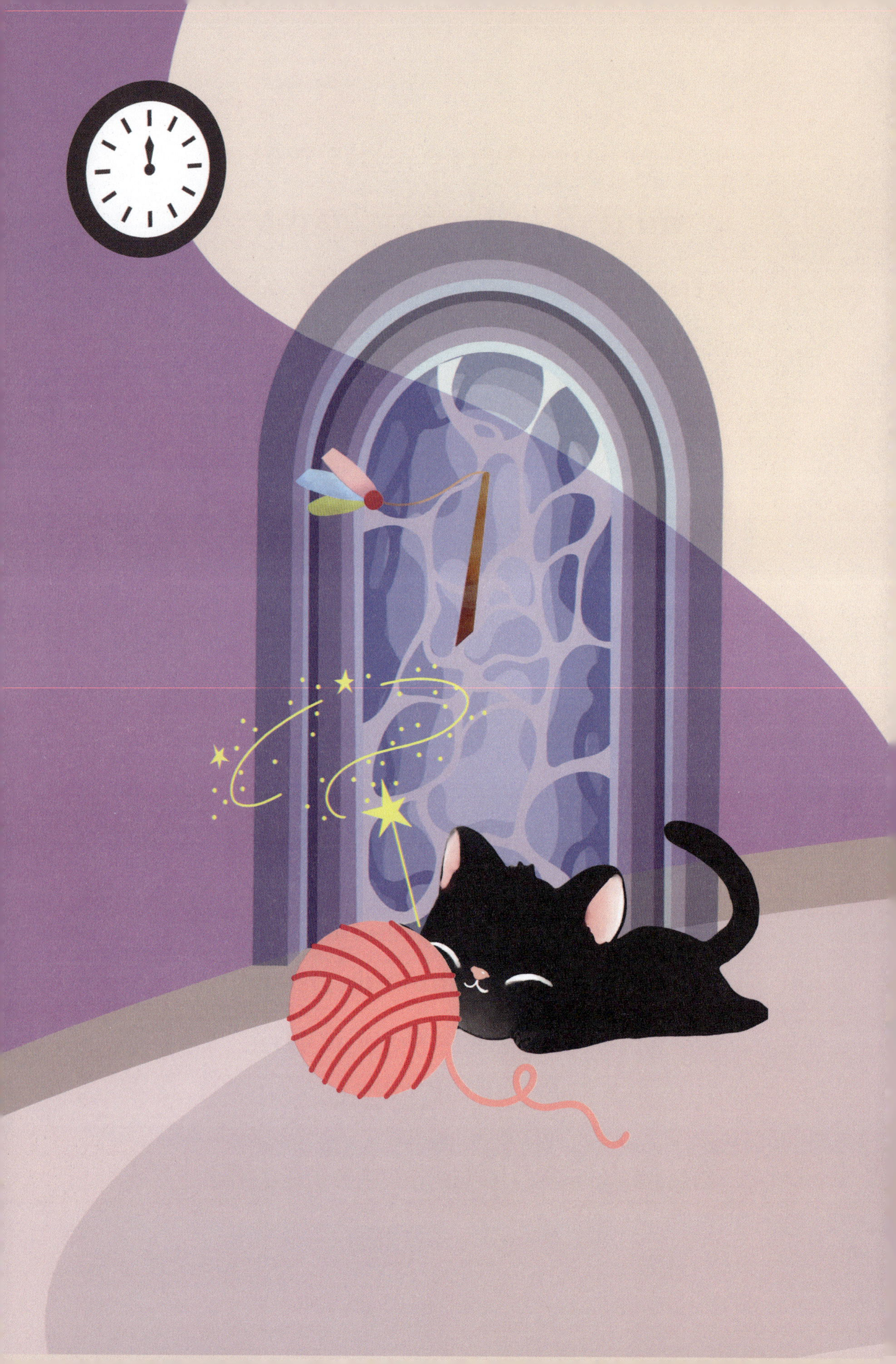

The wand glows, illuminating with sparkles, as the magic bursts into reality! Minnie discovers where she will adventure as it explodes in a puff of glitter.

Activate the magical wand with Minnie with three taps.
ONE TWO THREE!!!
On the final tap.....

Minnie landed on the MOON. She could feel the bumpy rocks tickle against her paws as she tumbled into landing with BANG!

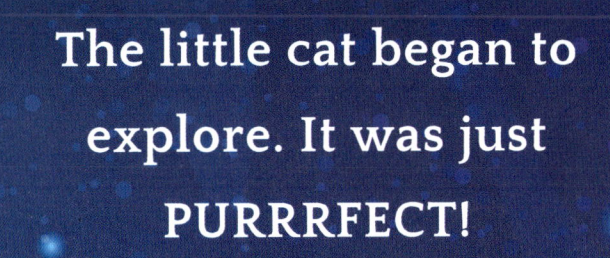

The little cat began to explore. It was just PURRRFECT!

Minnie twirled around in excitement. A group of aliens whizzed by, surfing through the cosmos.

The little cat waved at the aliens and asked, "Do you have space for one more? I'm on a magical adventure, and surfing looks like a magical way to explore."

"Of course!" replied the aliens. "Hop on board"

Minnie jumped on to the shiny purple board, the little cat soared and whirled around the moon. A beautiful shooting star flew past, it really was MAGICAL.

Soon, it was time for Minnie to continue her adventure. She thanked the friendly aliens for making her feel so welcome and then took off in search of her magical wand.

Minnie tapped her magical wand three times... and with a puff of smoke, She found herself diving into the beautiful blue ocean.

Her fur was as soft as velvet as she leaped into the waves! The little cat swam alongside mermaids whose shimmering tails sparkled in the sunlight. Their hair flowed like silk, swirling gracefully through the water.

It was truly enchanting! Molly the mermaid displayed her best swimming talents for Minnie. "Do you have any tricks in the water?" Molly asked as she elegantly swam through the waves. "I do! I'm a magical cat who can dance in the water," Minnie replied, showcasing her most impressive twirl.

Molly giggled with joy, " come with me I can show you more of the beautiful ocean ". The friends swam off together and in that magical moment they became the best of friends!!

After a fun day, it was time to say goodbye. Minnie had more exploring to do. Where do you think she will travel to next?

Minnie flew across the sky in a ball of shimmering magic, before gently touching down on the soft, fluffy snow of the North Pole.

"Hello", called out a deep voice. It was Mr. Frosty the Snowman. He stood tall and proud ,wearing a smart top hat and a cosy scarf. The Penguin's played happily by his side.

The air was crisp and the sun was beaming in the sky. It was the perfect time to explore. " Hello, would you kindly show me around the mountains ? I'm on a magical adventure. I would love to share it with friends".

Frosty was not keen on adventures. He preferred to stay in the one spot! Do not worry. I have a magical wand that can rescue us if we get stuck. With some nudges of encouragement, Frosty agreed and off they went!

The friends stayed close together as they explored. They saw a beautiful narwhale swim in the water and a white polar bear chilling by the side.

Minnie's favorite animal was the magnificent white polar bear. His fur shimmered glistening under the bright sun—truly enchanting.

Frosty suddenly let out a scream, startling everyone in the group. A snowy owl swooped down just above his head, nearly knocking his hat from his head!

"It's getting quite dark; should we make our way back down the mountain?" asked the littlest penguin. Before the friends could respond, the little penguin was already back at the icy igloo, snuggling in for the evening!

As the sky grew darker it was time for Minnie to say goodbye to her friends " I will visit you all again soon" said Minnie as she activated her wand and flew away into the starlit sky.

Minnie has made a stop in Paris! Before she heads home, "Oh la la!" said the little cat, "It's time for some of my favorite pizza; my tummy is rumbling!"

Minnie enjoyed her delicious pizza while watching the world go by. It was the perfect way to end her magical journey.

With a full belly, Minnie
was ready to go home.

The little cat waved her magical
wand and flew through the sky
in a swirl of magical dust.

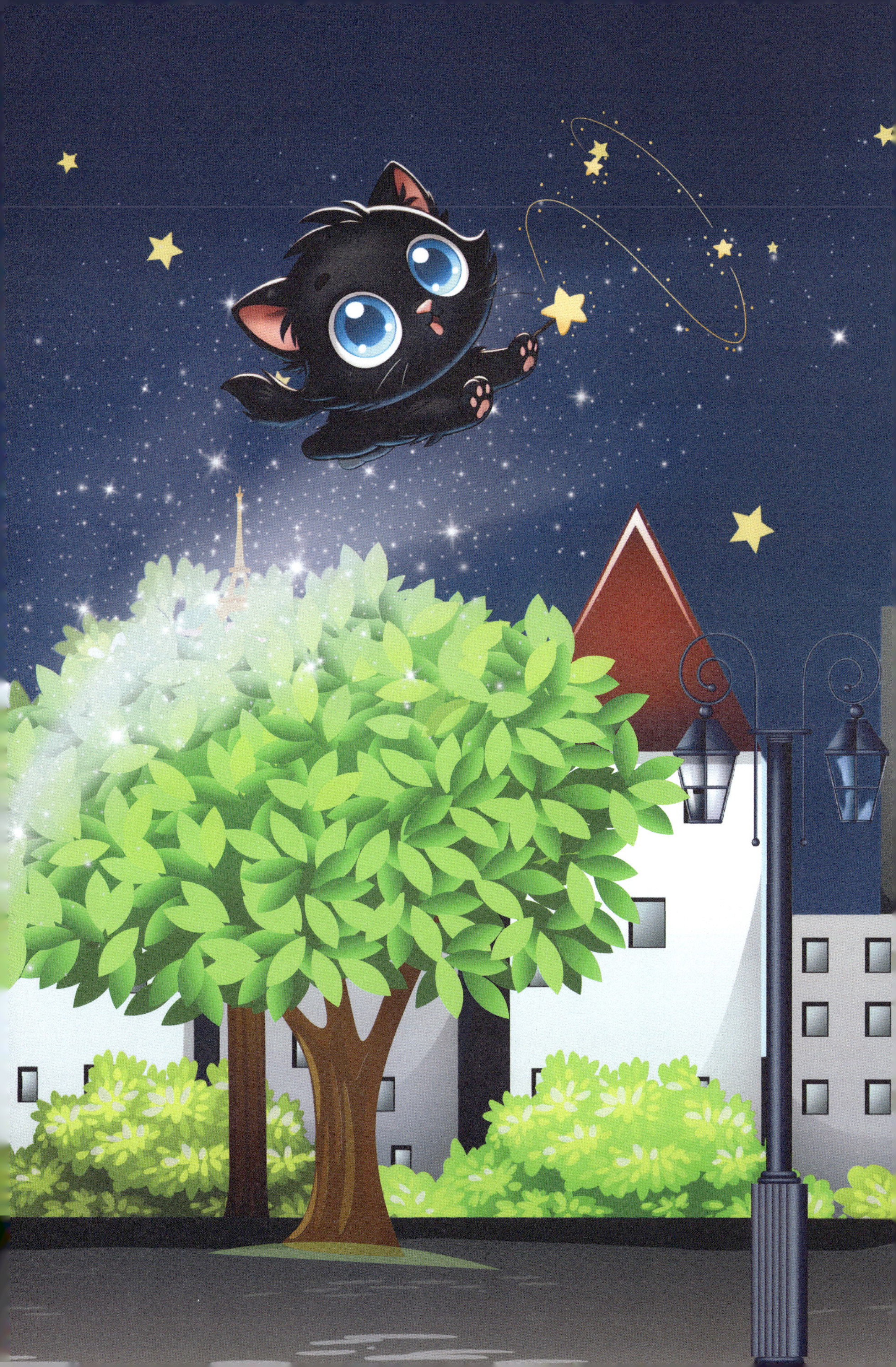

She soon reached home. Minnies family were so happy to see her, they wanted to know all about her enchanting adventure. "Will you be going away again soon"? Asked the family.

"I'm already dreaming up my next adventure with my best friend, Molly the Mermaid. I will tell you more tomorrow, I'm very sleepy after all the magic"!

And the little cat said "good night sweet dreams" as she curled up in her bed and drifted off to sleep

The end.

Printed in Great Britain
by Amazon